THE POCKET
UNIVERSAL
PRINCIPLES OF
ARCHITECTURE

THE POCKET
UNIVERSAL
PRINCIPLES OF
ARCHITECTURE

**100 Architectural Archetypes,
Methods, Conditions, Relationships,
and Imaginaries**

**Nathalie Frankowski & Cruz Garcia
WAI Architecture Think Tank**

ROCKPORT

Quarto.com

© 2025 Quarto Publishing Group USA Inc.
Text © 2025 Cruz Garcia and Nathalie Frankowski / WAI Architecture Think Tank
Images © 2025 Cruz Garcia and Nathalie Frankowski / WAI Architecture Think Tank

First published in 2025 by Rockport Publishers, an imprint of The Quarto Group,
100 Cummings Center, Suite 265-D, Beverly, MA 01915, USA.
T (978) 282-9590 F (978) 283-2742 Quatro.com

Rockport Publishers titles are also available at discount for retail, wholesale, promotional, and bulk purchase. For details, contact the Special Sales Manager by email at specialsales@quarto.com or by mail at The Quarto Group, Attn: Special Sales Manager, 100 Cummings Center, Suite 265-D, Beverly, MA 01915, USA.

10 9 8 7 6 5 4 3 2 1

ISBN: 978-0-7603-9380-2

Digital edition published in 2025
eISBN: 978-0-7603-9381-9

Library of Congress Cataloging-in-Publication Data is available

Text:
Cruz Garcia & Nathalie Frankowski,
WAI Architecture Think Tank

Images:
Cruz Garcia & Nathalie Frankowski,
WAI Architecture Think Tank

Printed in China

To worldmaking emancipatory futures

and to Ema Yuizarix . . .

CONTENTS

INTRODUCTION

 ## ARCHETYPES

■ ## METHODS

CONDITIONS

 RELATIONSHIPS

� IMAGINARIES

INTRODUCTION

The Pocket Universal Principles of Architecture is a compendium of the strategies, processes, worldviews, ambitions, materials, and challenges that shape and are shaped by architecture. Designed as a small travel guide to the vast terrain of the architectural imagination, the book expands to a broader public a much-needed conversation about the importance, possibilities, and role that architecture plays in our lives. The book is a reflection on how spaces—from the intimate interiors of a room, a house, or an apartment to the buildings that make the urban fabric of cities and town—not only determine a great portion of our interactions with one another and the environment but are also present in the ways we think and interact with the world. *The Pocket Universal Principles of Architecture* engages not only with the material manifestations of architecture—the wood, brick and mortar, concrete, and steel—but with the immaterial realm of ideas, concepts, perceptions, and sensibilities.

The book expands and challenges preconceptions about both, the word "architecture" and the concept of the universal to delve into an accessible and imaginative approach at understanding and grasping the spatial, material, and worldmaking practices that facilitate different forms of designed mediations with the environment. With a focus on a pluralistic, inclusive, and accessible idea about universality, the book proposes a list of one hundred principles of architecture that are inclusive, comprehensive, critical, imaginative, and (extra)planetary.

Structure of the book

The Pocket Universal Principles of Architecture is divided into five parts, each one containing twenty principles that can be read in any order. Each part in the book engages with architecture at different scales and stages of the design process, from the initial ideas to reflections on the effects of the built environment, to architectural desires and aspirations to transform the world.

● *Archetypes* deals with organizing concepts and ideas after which architecture is molded. ■ *Methods* focuses on the intersection of media, materials, representation, and design planning, building, and unbuilding processes. ▲ *Conditions* refers to phenomena that arise out of contextual, ecological, political, social, and cultural characteristics. ◆ *Relationships* highlights sensorial, bodily, social, and ecological interactions with architecture. ✱ *Imaginaries* provides a lens to look, imagine, analyze, and speculate future architectural conditions in and beyond the world.

Each principle in the book is accompanied by an image composed using the collage (26) method. These images provide visual narrative support to each of the principles. The combination of text and images makes this book similar to architecture as a practice and a way of thinking that should be both accessible and expansive. We hope that the readers of *The Pocket Universal Principles of Architecture* find a useful resource to engage with a world that is shaped by architecture, and by architectures that are in turn transformed by social, political, cultural, ecological, and philosophical forces.

VOLUMETRIC ARCHETYPES
Architectures of pure geometric forms and their combinations

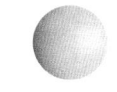

Types
Cubes are shapes, either solid or hollow, contained by six quadrilaterals of similar size.

Spheres are constructions that appear circular in elevation.

Pyramids are geometric forms with a polygonal base and sloping sides, meeting at an apex.

Cones consist of solid or hollow artifacts tapering from a circular or roughly circular base to a point.

Cylinders consist of a solid form with two parallel, congruent circular or oval bases connected by a lateral surface.

Applications
Volumetric Archetypes can be designed individually or in groups of the same shape or different shapes. They can be the starting point for more detailed and specific designs, be part of larger systems, or become urban conditions.

2
SPATIAL ARCHETYPES
Design by addition, subtraction, and other strategies of space

Types
Addition consists of attaching forms or elements to an existing space.

Subtraction is the process of removing certain elements from a design to create a new effect in the space.

Penetration consists of the insertion of volumes or spaces inside other volumes or spaces.

Divisions are elements or spatial effects that create a sense of discontinuity or separation within a design.

Space-in-space creates spaces within other, bigger spaces such an enclosed room inside an open room or vice versa.

Compression and expansion consist of creating narrow, constricting, and intimate spaces that lead to more open, spacious, and tall spaces.

Applications
An architectural project can include some or all of these spatial archetypes.

3
ORGANIZATIONAL ARCHETYPES
Architectures of centrality, axiality, networks, layering, and stacking

Types

Centrality consists on the placement of a dominant space or element in the center of design.

Axiality addresses the clear visual, spatial, or physical connection between elements or spaces.

Networks are underlying systems of interconnected elements.

Layering creates, by means of elements or spaces, a series or sequence.

Stacking implies the piling up of volumes, spaces, or artifacts.

Applications

Although organizational archetypes are not definite, centrality, axiality, networks, layering, and stacking can and have been used in different combinations. Each of these archetypes can be applied at different scales, from the domestic to the urban.

4
SQUARE ARCHETYPES
Closed, nuclear, dominated, grouped, and amorphous open spaces

Types

Closed squares are enclosed areas of varying sizes surrounded by urban fabric or structures.

Nuclear squares are open spaces containing an object, artifact, monument, or structure.

Dominated squares contain an imponent architectural artifact of significant symbolism or size.

Grouped squares result from the combination of several open forms.

Amorphous squares are open spaces that are not clearly defined.

Applications

Squares don't have to be square in shape. Different factors like the scale of squares and their accessibility, openness, visibility, shading, or heating, as well as the programs of the surrounding structures, will determine if a square has a positive effect on its context.

MEGALITHIC ARCHETYPES
Dolmens, menhirs, inukshuks, and other structures in stone

Types

Dolmens are single-chamber structures that include portal or simple dolmens; great dolmens; polygonal dolmens; and rectangular, enlarged, or extended dolmens.

Inukshuks consist of large stacked stones in a vertical or anthropomorphic composition used by indigenous peoples in the Arctic to navigate, mark sacred places, or demarcate the land.

Menhirs are large, upright stones that are used as monuments or markers.

Cairns are piles of stones, typically used as markers or memorials.

Applications

While the documentation of the construction of historical iterations of megalithic archetypes is not conclusive, new construction technologies could enhance alternative stone compositions and structures on a different scale and with a wide variety of uses.

6
VITRUVIAN ARCHETYPES
Order, composition, decorum, proportion, symmetry, and economy

Types
Ordering is the proportion of the components of a project, individually and as part of an overall scheme.

Composition accounts for the arrangement of all parts of the building and its pleasing effects.

Decorum or *correctness* implies a form of appropriateness of the building to function or tradition.

Proportion is the perceived harmony between the parts of a building.

Symmetry arises from proportion, a due adjustment of the size of the different parts to each other and to the whole.

Economy consists of the efficient management of resources and of the site, as well as the principled supervision of project management.

Applications
According to these principles, firmness (withstanding elements), utility (function and comfort), and delight (aesthetics and pleasurable experiences) are all essential for creating enduring and enjoyable spaces.

FIGURATIVE ARCHETYPES
Forms and shapes that are representative of something else

Types

Responsive figuration relies on the form or shape of the structure to explicitly communicate its use or program.

Autonomous figuration takes place when the program, function, or use of a building is unrelated to its figurative form.

Applications

Figurative archetypes have been called *architecture parlante* ("talking architecture") to identify many French architectures of the eighteenth century, or "ducks" (in reference to the Big Duck building in Long Island, New York) by designer Robert Venturi. Some of the purposes of figurative archetypes include making the building more easily recognizable, creating a symbol that communicates its uses, or using architecture to act as a communication device where structures engage with whoever is observing the building.

HARDCORIST ARCHETYPES

Architecture designed as pure formal exploration

Types
Inverted pyramids are structures that give the impression of a pyramid turned upside down.

Blow-up fonts, or urban typography, are structures that spell either individual letters when alone or abbreviations or complete names when put together.

Speleothems resemble mineral formations that are never identical to each other but resemble each other enough to be considered a group.

Stacked boxes are structures made with volumes that appear to be resting on top of or next to one another.

Loops connect two towers at the ground and top levels, creating a visually continuous looping form or Möbius strip.

Applications
Whether to create singular symbols with cultural meaning or to display a cluster of structures that showcase economic, social, and political power, hardcorist archetypes have been used during different moments in history. As material science, engineering, and construction methods continue to advance, new hardcorist archetypes become feasible.

FIVE POINTS
Designing pilotis, roof gardens, free plans, ribbon windows, and free facades

Types

Pilotis raise a building off the ground to bring more space and light underneath.

Roof gardens, or terraces, are flat roofs that can be systematically used.

Free plans take advantage of the pilotis in the ground plan that form a building's support system as all interior divisions of the space may be placed freely according to functional or aesthetic needs.

Ribbon windows, or horizontal fenestrations, allow light into all rooms and create a more open feeling within a building. They are made possible by the lack of structural walls.

Free facades mean that designers are no longer constrained by traditional architectural rules when designing the exterior of buildings, allowing them to be more expressive in their work.

Applications

While the five points were written with a specific aesthetic in mind, the relationship between industrial methods of production and construction processes continue to be relevant today through their different combinations and uses in buildings of different scales, and in different programs beyond housing.

10
NONSOLID ARCHITECTURES
Architectures that are not made of conventionally solid materials

Types
Physical nonsolid architectures create spatial conditions using unconventional materials, mostly in liquid or gaseous states. These structures often need the support of additional building components that will regulate characteristics such as air and humidity pressure, air or water flows, condensation, precipitation, and light intensity.

Experiential nonsolid architectures are structures and spaces that promote sensorial interactions that go beyond visual characteristics. Some of these architectures are produced by designing for the experience of sounds, smells, and thermal conditions, or their combination.

Applications
Some experimental reasons for nonsolid architectures may include designing spaces that have a tangible and recognizable form but that may not leave a lasting footprint on a given site. On the other hand, some of the practical applications for nonsolid architectures can include creating spaces for different forms of sensibilities and (nonvisual) ways to experience the world.

VOID
Carved, dug, buried, and other forms of architectural subtraction

Types
Face rock voids consist of architectures carved out of the rock of mountain slopes and cliffs. These voids can be designed as original structures or inhabit existing infrastructures such as mines, aqueducts, and tunnels.

Underground voids are architectures made by removing earth and rocks from below the ground. These underground voids may provide spaces for occupation without visually disrupting a site.

Applications
The mass of void structures can have a beneficial effect on the regulation of the temperature inside the spaces. Void archetypes can provide protection from atmospheric and environmental phenomena, as well as satisfy cultural or mythological narratives about living inside the mountains or under the ground.

All across the world, from the Longmen Grottoes in China to the temples in Lalibela, Ethiopia, to the Puebloan cliff dwellings in the United States, architectures have been carved, dug, and sculpted on the ground, in the face of mountains, and across large rock formations.

ORNAMENT
Decoration in the facades, structures, and interiors of architecture

Types
Facade ornament can be used to create a visual language that communicates the narratives or values of a given culture or to act as a technical regulator of the environmental conditions of the building. For example, ornamentation can help deflect sunlight or regulate ventilation.

Structural ornament, or ornamental elements on the structure of a building, can serve a number of purposes, including hiding imperfections, reinforcing the structure, or adding affective elements.

Interior ornament in the elements of a building like floors, walls, and ceilings can give character to the space or reflect the culture, history, or aesthetic values of a person, group, or place. Interior ornament can also be achieved by means of artifacts like lamps, fixtures, and receptacles.

Applications
While ornamentation has been closely linked to intensive labor practices, new technologies of construction, assembly, production, and customization can play a role in the incorporation and possible applications, and combinations of functional forms of ornament in architecture.

MEGASTRUCTURE
Very big terrestrial, aquatic, flying, cosmic, and extraplanetary structures

Types

Terrestrial megastructures are cities inside buildings that are anchored or moving on land.

Aquatic megastructures are colossal structures containing a vast number of programs either floating or submerged under the sea.

Flying megastructures are structures capable of flying or floating in the air that are large enough to contain the diverse programs of a city.

Cosmic megastructures are large artificial structures that have been built in space including Dyson spheres, ringworlds, and Matrioshka brains.

Extraplanetary megastructures are large, artificially conditioned structures that are built on other planets.

Applications

Megastructures have all the necessary amenities and utilities of a city contained within the boundaries of a single architectural form. Today, megastructures could respond to urgent questions like population growth, climate change, environmental pollution, and energy consumption.

SUPER TALL
**Structures, buildings, and spaces
reaching extraordinary heights**

Types

Supertall buildings are buildings that are between about 1,000 and 2,000 feet (305 m and 610 m). The design of supertall buildings has to account for many challenges, including their high cost, the difficulty of evacuating them in an emergency, and the incredible pressure of winds at such heights.

Megatall buildings are taller than 2,000 feet (605 m). While only a few of these incredibly tall towers have been constructed, many of them are part of ideal-city plans by architects, planners, and politicians. Megatall buildings are also at the center of many science fiction stories.

Applications

As technology, material science, and structural engineering advance, and political and financial powers find ways to be consolidated, development groups seem to be in a global contest to build the tallest tower. While supertall or megatall buildings are feats of technological innovation, due to their high cost and the amount of energy and material needed to construct them, these projects very rarely address ecological challenges or social problems such as affordable or social housing.

STEALTH
**Architectures of disappearance,
disguise, and camouflage**

Types
Disappearing architectures use mechanical, environmental, or technical features
to make a building or structure completely invisible.

Disguise architectures use a variety of techniques to make a structure blend in
with its surroundings. Some strategies include designing external shells that
simulate different programs to the ones contained inside the building.

Camouflage architectures are designed to conceal a structure, usually by
blending it in with its surroundings. This can be done by using color, pattern,
and textures; growing organic matter on its facade; or coating the structure
with special materials that disrupt cameras or satellite images.

Applications
Some contemporary applications of stealth architecture include the use of
radar-absorbent materials, special paint finishes, and unique shapes and angles
to help reduce the visibility of a structure to radar. This type of architecture is
often used for military buildings and other sensitive structures where it is
important to reduce the risk of detection.

BLOB
Amorphous, shapeless, and irregularly shaped architectures

Types
Ancestral blobs are amorphous structures that have been historically built with locally sourced materials and construction techniques. These structures can be found all around the world and include architectures built with clay, dirt, straw, rocks, and ice.

High-tech blobs are amorphous structures that incorporate computer-aided design (CAD) or advanced computing software and materials in their design and construction. These blobs can be made of soft materials such as silicone, rubber, or gel. They can be inflatable or use custom-made facade materials, such as ceramics, fibers, or even plastic.

Applications
Because of their undefined or even malleable forms, blobs can host a wide variety of programs, provide endless aesthetic options, and can be designed for extremely different environments and climates. They can be used at different scales, from furniture to follies to museums to housing. Because they can be built with different materials, blobs can be constructed on land, in water, or even in the air.

17
TOPO ARCHITECTURE

Buildings, structures, and spaces that are also landscape

Types

Aesthetic topo architectures re-create the form and looks of parks and follow the stylistic characteristics of a landscape rather than its function, maintenance, or uses. Some examples include buildings with trees inside or on the roof.

Functional topo architectures are concerned with the performance of a building or structure. These projects emulate or become part of landscapes to create special ways to circulate through the building or to use natural components to regulate temperature, illumination, smells, ventilation, and even maintenance.

Applications

Although the relationship between architecture and landscape can be traced back to the beginnings of many civilizations, today architects and designers pursue topographic buildings for many reasons. Some of these may include to create unique designs that bring nature into urban settings or to re-earth cities or make cities greener, to take spatial or ecological advantage of natural materials or features, or to further improve the energy efficiency of buildings.

PARASITIC ARCHITECTURE

Structures attached to or protruding from other buildings

Types
Appendix parasites are structural interventions that provide additional programs or utilities to an already existing structure.

Insertion parasites are visible only from the interior of a building. They may consist of new spaces, rooms, or structures suspended from ceilings or walls.

Bubbles are transparent or translucent structures containing new spaces.

Clusters are groups of parasitic architecture that create a system outside or inside of an already existing structure.

Applications
Contemporary iterations of parasitic architectures may be used to address current pressing issues, including using experimental materials that would be too costly or risky at the total scale of a building; providing small-scale samples of self-sustaining systems that can provide food, water, and shelter for people in need; providing spaces to share with nonhuman species; creating climatic bubbles; or experimenting with alternative forms of living.

19

INFRASTRUCTURAL ARCHITECTURE

Buildings that are also bridges, tunnels, and other forms of utilities

Types

Highway architectures are linear cities made up of buildings that provide multiple uses at the base of streets where cars, buses, and other forms of vehicular transit travel.

Tunnel architectures are the result of buildings assembled to cover pathways, railways, and streets.

Bridge architectures connect two or more structures together, suspended over a body of water, farmland, or another geographical or urban feature.

Ports are multipurpose buildings that are simultaneously a landing or anchoring pad for transportation vessels (airplanes, blimps, boats, submarines).

Applications

Because of their efficiency and more compact footprint, infrastructural architectures are planned to condense in a single structure all the programs that would usually be associated with large-scale infrastructure projects. Some examples are ideal urban plans that propose the elimination of urban sprawl, and the concentration of all living programs in a single, continuous building.

20

BIG BOX
Very large buildings contained inside a single-facade envelope

Types

Fun palaces are buildings with transformable interiors that are intended for entertainment purposes.

Icons are big boxes that serve a symbolic role.

Data centers can vary greatly in terms of their size, layout, and features, and can include raised floors, cooling systems, and backup power generators.

Mechanical boxes conceal technical utilities, such as water treatment plants, condensation units, power and relay stations, or waste management facilities.

Sarcophagi are massive steel and concrete structures covering toxic or nuclear sites. This type of big box is a confinement structure that is built to contain hazardous materials.

Applications

Some contemporary applications of big box buildings include storage facilities, warehouses, and distribution centers. These types of buildings are often designed for functionality and efficiency, and their lack of windows helps minimize heat loss and maximize security.

MANIFESTOS

**Compelling declarations of a
vision, intent, goal, or mission**

Types

Individual manifestos emphasize the beliefs, values, or intentions of a singular
author, designer, or architect.

Collective manifestos are produced by groups to outline their shared beliefs,
values, or intentions.

Centralized manifestos are statements made by individuals or collectives who
assume that a set of beliefs, values, or intentions should be taken as the norm.
This type of manifesto positions the authors at the center of the future.

Decentralized manifestos are documents that imagine a future that may not
include their authors. In this type of manifesto, architects or designers may
remove themselves from any vision of the future.

Retroactive manifestos outline the goals and principles of a movement or
organization after the fact.

Applications

Whether as rules to follow, goals to achieve, or obstacles to overcome,
manifestos, which can be in the form of books, exhibitions, or even as built
projects, play an important role in architecture, ecology, and society today.

22
DIAGRAMMING
Highlighting architecture's basic functions, layout, and programs

Types

Programmatic diagrams portray how different functions and uses are distributed within the layout of a project. These diagrams can represent programs through forms, colors, or texts.

Flow diagrams outline or simulate paths created by moving components, including people, animals, automobiles, air, and water.

Form diagrams display how the shape of a building, landscape, or territory affect and are affected by other nonformal conditions.

Time-based diagrams layer in a single drawing, or a series of schemes, how spaces, flows, actions, and interactions occur in a given space over time.

Applications

Architectural diagrams are illustrations or graphic representations that demonstrate an array of concepts, principles, or information that aim to clarify the relationship between components and the overall design of a project. Diagrams can take many forms as they outline a project's concept by means of charts, lines, bubbles, arrows, and other graphic strategies. Diagrams can operate at different scales and focus on a wide range of subjects and concepts.

23

SKETCHING
Drawing the basic outline, main ideas, or concepts of a project

Types
Individual sketching consists of portraying ideas, forms, or design suggestions by a sole author or designer.

Collective sketching considers the participation of several designers in the outlining of a collaborative drawing or design. Some examples of collective sketching include cadavre exquis (see 35), where a drawing or representation is continued without modification by a group.

Applications
While sketching has been part of architectural design for a long time, new digital mediums and design softwares have unlocked the possibility of digital sketching. These new forms of sketching can be done individually, in the form of a collective, or even automated, as design scripts can be given as input to computers while artificial intelligence software generates sketches out of those prompts (see 77). As new technologies emerge, rather than being substituted by them, sketching continues to be an essential method of architectural design.

24

MODELING
Constructing the three-dimensional representation of a design

Types

Physical modeling is the process of creating a three-dimensional representation of a building, structure, space, or site, usually on a smaller scale.

Digital modeling is the process of creating a digital representation of a design or condition, usually using computer software.

Conceptual modeling focuses on the fundamental ideas of a design, usually in the form of an abstract or simplified model.

Detailed modeling is the representation of accurate and developed parts of a design or complete project.

Mock-ups are 1:1 scale models accurately constructed.

Applications

As technology develops, models of artifacts, cities, landscapes, and events can be developed with increasing material and environmental accuracy, often being complemented with simulation software and three-dimensional printing construction techniques (see 38).

25

MASSING
**Three-dimensional volumetric
explorations of a project**

Types
Simple massings are tridimensional explorations of basic geometric forms or
design operations. This type of massing study can be used for the design of
regular buildings, urban conditions, and artifacts, or for the exploration of
specific design details.

Complex massings involve the use of unconventional techniques and tools to
create intricate shapes or details. While some well-documented complex
massing has been done by hanging weights on upside-down textiles to generate
the shape of vaults, contemporary parametric modeling, using algorithms and
scripting, can be used to create accurate, responsive massing models and
precise prototypes.

Applications
The process of massing can achieve several outcomes, including volumetric
(see 1) and hardcorist (see 8) forms, as well as much more complex shapes
and formal combinations, such as blobs (see 16) and topographical variations.
Massing can be achieved through many actions including adding, accumulating,
piling, and stacking, as well as cutting, removing, melting, and twisting.

26

COLLAGE
Image produced by the combination of other images

Types
Montage, or photomontage, is a type of collage in which an image or photo is edited to insert or remove elements.

Juxtaposition is a type of collage that aims to create a new image by pasting different images or elements into one composition.

Assemblage is the combination of different elements in space.

Applications
Collages can be used at different stages of the design process, from the initial conceptual phase to the presentation of a detailed design, and even to accompany the ideal visions of utopian manifestos (see 21 and 81). While many original collages produced manually use materials like paper, fabric, photographs, or objects, today, designers can produce digital collages, moving images, and animations in the computer with a high level of precision and realism with the use of photo editing and design software.

27

NARRATIVE ARCHITECTURE

Storytelling of architectural situations, conditions, and critiques

Types

Utopian narratives employ storytelling devices to create alluring images about ideal societies and projects. This type of narrative architecture is optimistic: It assigns a positive, life-changing role to the design of buildings and cities.

Kynical narratives operate in the form of subversion or critique. Instead of elaborating stories that invite, these narrative architectures create doubt and questions, or help outline problems that relate to architecture.

Applications

While being a central part of architectural discussions since the early 1970s, today narrative architecture can be used to engage with many of the pressing social and ecological challenges. If a utopian narrative explains how a skyscraper in the center of the city provides the most amazing, beautiful, and clear views for those who live there, a kynical narrative would question: Who gets left out? Who builds that architecture? How is ecology affected by building it? While utopian narratives create compelling stories, kynical narratives ask, "Whose utopia?"

28

KIT-OF-PARTS
**Design with predetermined
components and elements**

Types
Design kits-of-parts consist of elements that are used during the design portion of a project. This conceptual kit-of-parts is employed to help designers test configurations, layouts, and combinations of predetermined artifacts, objects, or elements.

Interactive kits-of-parts consist of predesigned, prefabricated, or preassembled elements inserted into a virtual or physical space intended for people to rearrange them. This form of kit-of-parts gives people the power to alter the spatial layout of architectural elements without having to incur permanent changes to immovable or structural elements.

Applications
Kits-of-parts are design tools that can benefit designers at all stages, from children learning about composition to practicing architects, interior and landscape designers, and urbanists designing at different scales and levels of detail and complexity. In their multiple variations, kits-of-parts can be used with predetermined instructions and guidelines, or just through pure spontaneity.

29

TACTICAL URBANISM
Punctual and specific urban interventions that are part of a larger plan

Types
Street plans consist of the reclaiming of the street for pedestrian purposes. Through the use of furniture, paint, and design elements, streets made for cars can be transformed for the use of the community, children, bikes, and more.

Urban pockets is a tactical strategy that repurposes discarded lots in a city or town and turns them into spaces for the community. Some examples include community gardens, playgrounds, outdoor cinemas, pools, skate parks, outdoor community classrooms, and social condensers (see 67).

Reclaimed infrastructure refurbishes empty buildings for collective, communal uses, including community pantries and kitchens, and communal daycare.

Applications
Without relying on centralized-planning decisions or big funding opportunities, tactical urbanism allows different types of organizations and the public at-large to lead neighborhood-improving design interventions across space and time.

30

PSYCHO-GEOGRAPHIC CARTOGRAPHIES

**Assembling urban experiences
with unexpected spatial combinations**

Types

Dérive ("drift") is a spontaneous exploration of a city, allowing oneself to be guided by chance encounters and the environment rather than a planned route.

Homo-ludens, or "human the player," is based on a theory that recognizes the importance of different forms of play in interactions between humans and one another, and with their environments. When applied to the scale of the city, the possibility, necessity, and right to play has the opportunity to reshape the urban experience.

Applications

Learning from the work of situationist planners and artists, psycho-geographic cartography is a method of reconstructing a place by the influence of people's feelings and behaviors. A form of counterplanning, it involves exploring cities without a plan, letting chance encounters shape the experience. This approach challenges traditional urban planning by focusing on human interaction and emotion rather than physical structures.

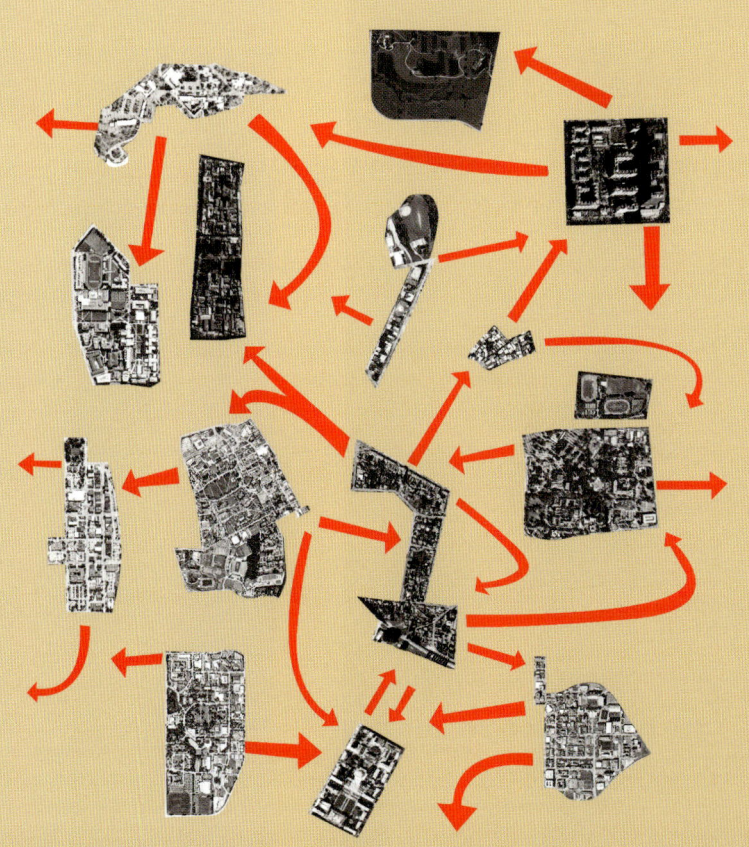

31

MAPPING
Outlining the conditions and characteristics behind a design project

Types

Thematic mapping emphasizes overall subjects, concepts, or narratives affecting an area of study. Some of the concepts of thematic mapping include social, political, economic, or ecological themes and their combinations.

Attribute mapping displays characteristics of a given space, site, image, or study. This type of mapping highlights inherent, evident, or hidden features, elements, systems of a site, space, or structure.

Experimental mapping responds to alternative self-generated processes developed by designers or collectives. Some examples of experimental mapping include psycho-geographic cartographies (see 30), decolonial maps, and mental maps.

Applications

Mapping is a versatile tool used for designing, analyzing, visualizing, and storytelling. It aids collaboration and decision-making among designers, communities, and policymakers. Different mapping techniques can be applied to various scales, from cities to buildings, and even abstract concepts like processes and data analysis strategies.

32

INVESTIGATIVE ARCHITECTURE
Identifying and researching various aspects of the built environment

Types

Territorial investigation is the process of gathering information about an area or location to understand events that may have taken place there.

Spatial investigation uses simulation and spatial design to focus on the analysis of actions and events taking place and their manifestations in space.

Material investigation deals with knowledge about materials and their properties. This type of research can be used to determine things like the health or ecological consequences of building materials on its users.

Applications

Combining journalism, forensic processes and technologies, and methods of architectural thinking and representation, investigative architecture focuses on the examination of social, environmental, and political issues. It can be used to study environmental disasters, like oil spills, to figure out what caused them, how long they've been happening, and how to fix them. It can also give a voice to oppressed peoples who are often ignored by showing their stories.

33

URBAN PATCHWORK
Designing smaller interactive spatial components (patches)

Types
Potential patches are in the process of becoming active by means of elements and interventions in a more or less delimited space.

Active patches are heterogeneous zones with semi-self-sustaining elements that contribute to the quality of one another.

Applications
Urban patchwork learns from an ecological method that pays close attention to how smaller ecological areas function and how they relate to each other on a grander scale. This method argues that the dynamics, relationships, and cycles of ecological systems can offer a valuable model for the self-sustenance of complex, heterogeneous, and lively areas and therefore contribute to the overall quality of spaces and interactions in a city. One of the key challenges of urban patchwork is to avoid exacerbating inequity within a space by means of displacement and gentrification, in the way that the slower development of the patches is paralleled with the protection of the communities that should be benefiting from them.

34

FIGURE-GROUND
Contrasting spatial differences of open and enclosed spaces

Types
Analytical figure-ground representations are used to understand the urban or spatial conditions of a place. When applied to towns, landscapes, cities, buildings, or structures, this mapping method can help determine the amount of mass or void space in an area, the shapes and forms, the scale, and the proximity of public or accessible space.

Speculative figure-ground compositions create designs by contrasting opposing spatial elements. Unlike traditional methods relying on data, this approach focuses on transforming the concepts of figure and ground into various design relationships.

Applications
Figure-ground is the process of abstracting the spatial conditions of a zone, space, land, or territory by representing contrasting conditions. A form of mapping (see 31), throughout history, figure-ground methods have been central to many urban theories that emphasize the importance of form in the operation of a city.

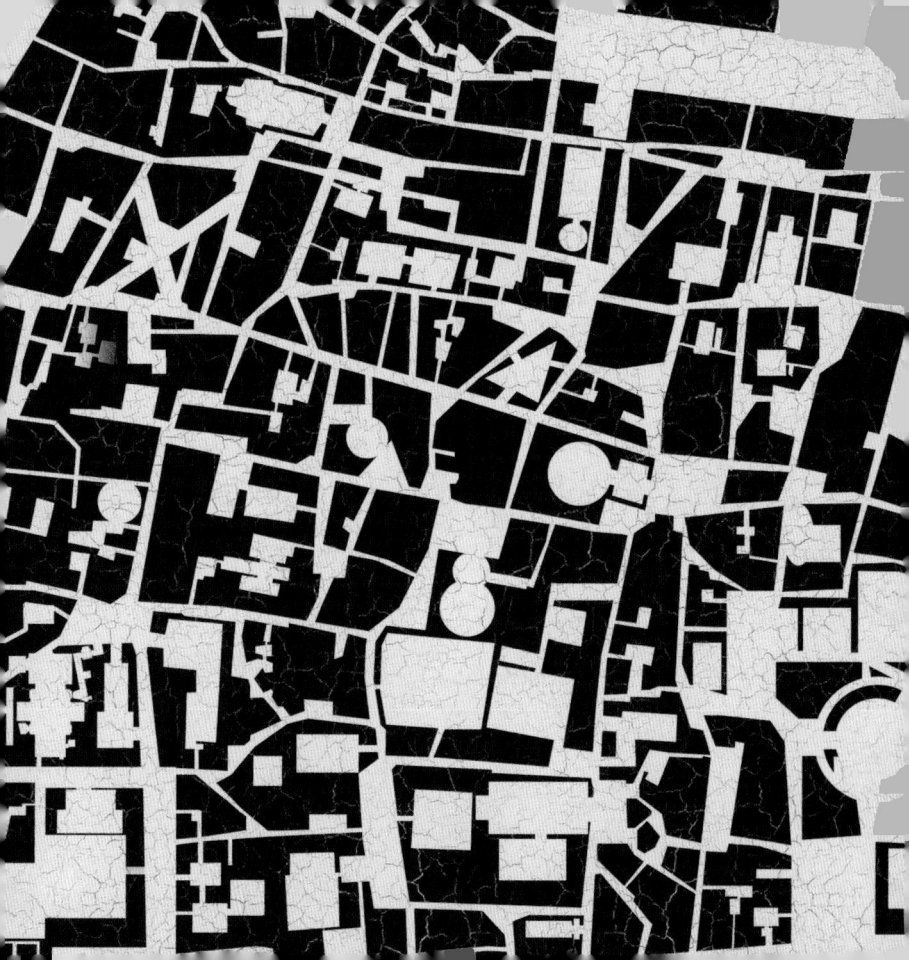

35

CADAVRE EXQUIS
Collective design where members don't know one another's input

Types
Drawing cadavre exquis is the closest application of the original surrealist exercise. It consists of participants drawing segments of a larger composition while completely ignoring what has been drawn before or by only revealing parts or all of the previous fragment. The rules of cadavre exquis are flexible and can be adapted depending on the desired outcome, the number of participants, or the type of drawing.

Multimedia cadavre exquis can be done by combining text, drawings, images, film, and objects. This type of collaborative method is similar to the drawing type, but instead of just relying on one tool of representation, it invites all the participants to reconsider the media being used.

Applications
With its origins in writing and drawing during the surrealist movement, cadavre exquis ("exquisite corpse") can be used for generating ideas for new buildings, urban layouts, or landscape designs and encouraging creativity and collaboration among architects, planners, designers, and people across disciplines.

36

MASH-UP
Combining disparate elements into a new design

Types
Collage mash-up is the process of merging different individual elements into a hybrid design that preserves parts of their original appearance. Like a collage, this type of mash-up is a mix of different styles or elements that remain identifiable even if their original use or concept has changed.

Blend mash-up fuses different individual elements into an unrecognizable new design. In this combination, all the individual elements become integral parts of a design. The final design of a blend mash-up will shift shapes in response to its components while maintaining an overall abstract form that doesn't reveal its initial characteristics.

Applications
While designers have created mash-ups throughout architectural history, new computer-aided design (CAD) and three-dimensional modeling software allows for new dynamic and interactive variations. Mashing up styles and elements can create unique designs and develop forms that adapt to various environmental, spatial, or functional needs.

37

PARAMETRIC
**Designing via the input
of parameters and variables**

Types
Analog parametric design is a method of devising parametric-responsive
structures, forms, or spaces using mathematical models and physical
experiments. Some examples include the study models that used gravity
and weights to determine the shape of vaults developed by Antoni Gaudi, the
tensile structures of the Olympic stadium in Munich designed by Frei Otto,
or New York's art deco setback towers.

Digital parametric design takes advantage of computational design software and
other digital applications that can simulate a real-time response to the input of
data and other parameters. This type of parametric design has been at the center
of many contemporary practices of architecture, fabrication, and design, as well
as in the network architectures of airports and train stations.

Applications
While a parametric architecture may try to consider all the conditioning
elements or parameters related to a project, this method relies on the freedom
of the architect or designer to decide how to use these parameters.

38

THREE-DIMENSIONAL PRINTING
Producing three-dimensional objects by means of machines

Types

Three-dimensional printing encompasses many manufacturing technologies that are capable of additively manufacturing objects, building components, and entire structures. Some examples of three-dimensional printing include stereolithography (SLA), selective laser sintering (SLS), fused deposition modeling (FDM), digital light process (DLP), Multi Jet Fusion (MJF), PolyJet direct metal laser sintering (DMLS), and electron beam melting (EBM).

Rapid prototyping is another form of additive manufacturing. Usually conducted during the process of design because of its fast fabrication, rapid prototyping produces studies of physical parts, models, or assembly. These studies can be done as accurately as possible in the form of high-fidelity prototypes, or as rough sketches or low-fidelity prototypes.

Applications

Three-dimensional printing can mass-produce building parts, create adaptable homes, and build in extreme environments. Its versatility and potential for remote operation make it suitable for space or underwater construction.

39

ROBOT FABRICATION

Constructing, assembling, and manufacturing projects with robots

Types

Stationary robots operate without moving their base. Including cable and gantry robots and robotic arms, these robots aid in the construction of artifacts, objects, or structures while anchored to the floor, ceiling, walls, or any other surface or support element.

Mobile robots can fabricate while moving by ground, air, or water. Swarm robots consist of networks of many small robots that can cooperate and perform tasks together. Like mobile robots, these systems can construct structures beyond their size and potentially work in tandem.

Applications

Among their many applications, robots can be used to build everything from study models and fast prototypes to complex structures and entire buildings. In combination with three-dimensional printing and other forms of additive manufacturing, robots can perform both simple and complex tasks and potentially repair and fabricate other robots.

40

LIVING ARCHITECTURE
Using living organisms as construction and spatial materials

Types

Living architectures are buildings, components, or design elements that incorporate biological processes or organisms. At the scale of components, some examples include self-healing materials, bacteria-based insulation, and heat-producing compost.

Living urbanism integrates the principles and methods of living architectures and applies them to the community scale. Living urbanism thinks of the city as an extension of nature and combines chemistry, biology, and design to think of public infrastructure and utilities as an integral part of life.

Applications

As climatic challenges become more pressing, new forms of living architecture can take advantage of technological advances and ancestral forms of ecological knowledge. Living architectures could grow, heal, and feed people; reuse and clean water; absorb pollutants and carbon dioxide; and cool down and warm up conditions. They propose to re-earth (return the earth back to) the city, bringing nature to some of the least sustainable and ecological spaces around the globe.

41

ECOLOGICAL ARCHITECTURE

**Buildings, spaces, and structures
in balance with nature**

Types

Green architecture focuses on using environmentally responsive materials
and energy-efficient design including vegetative roofs and walls, rainwater
harvesting, gray water recycling, solar and wind power.

Sustainable architecture takes into account the building's long-term impact
on the environment while considering its effects on society.

Applications

A truly sustainable architecture is concerned with not only factors that relate to
environmentally sound materials and the building's energy performance but also
the people and ecologies affected directly by it. An environmentally responsive
building that doesn't address people's needs is simply not sustainable. To
pursue forms of ecological architecture, designers should combine forms of
ancient knowledge, common sense, and critical understanding of a building
and its material, labor, site, and surroundings.

42

SPIRITUAL ARCHITECTURE

**Structures and spaces for
spiritual practices, rituals, and customs**

Types

Enclosed spiritual architectures are structures, buildings, enclosures, and
spaces designated for a spiritual practice or ritual. By means of building form,
construction details, types of ornament, design and spatial layouts, presence of
symbols, acoustic properties, and colors used, these spaces are designed to
promote reflection and contemplation and create a sense of introspection,
pedagogy, community, awe, or reverence.

Open spiritual architectures can be found in nature and cities, and can relate to
everything from mountains and forests to gardens and lakes to the sky and the
universe. These spaces, or spatial sequences, can be used for both personal and
communal meditation and prayer, and include landforms, burial mounds, ground
materials, or a composition or particular view framed on a landscape.

Applications

There are as many uses for spiritual architectures as there are people, cultures,
and belief systems. These designs can be focused on ancestral or modern, or
global or local spiritual practices.

43
MULTISENSORIAL ARCHITECTURE
Spaces for engaging with many senses and sensibilities

Types

Haptic architecture focuses on the sense of touch, using materials with varying textures and temperatures.

Aural architecture focuses on sound, using elements like water, wind, music, and vibrating materials.

Visual architecture focuses on sight, using bright colors, patterns, and unique shapes and formal combinations.

Olfactory architecture focuses on smell, using scented materials, plants, and other odor-producing elements.

Gustatory architecture focuses on taste, using edible elements and other flavorful features.

Applications

Through varying design strategies, multisensorial architecture combines sight, sound, touch, smell, and taste in its design.

44

CRITICAL SPATIAL PRACTICE

Spatial interventions that change or challenge social conventions

Types

Feminist critical spatial practices ensures that marginalized women, trans people, and nonbinary people are included in the design of architecture.

Democratic critical spatial practices are forms of social engagement that use space as a platform for critical dialogue and action.

Ecological critical spatial practices are practices that aim to protect and restore the environment for the benefit of humans and nonhumans.

Decolonial critical spatial practices aim to challenge Eurocentric or colonial narratives, engage in land reclamation projects, or create community-based planning initiatives for marginalized communities.

Applications

Critical spatial practice is a design method that challenges oppresive systems. As society faces growing challenges, this approach can evolve to address them.

45

SOCIAL JUSTICE DESIGN

Designing for social equity and fair conditions for people

Types
Accessibility is about creating spaces and buildings that everyone can use, regardless of their abilities. This includes involving people with different sensibilities, disabilities, and material conditions in the design process.

Prison abolition is a type of design predicated on the notion that in order for society to be fairer and just, it cannot rely on prisons and other forms of carceral punishment and control.

Social care design focuses on creating spaces like affordable housing, hospitals, parks, and playgrounds that improve people's well-being.

Reparative or restorative design focuses on fixing problems in society, especially those affecting marginalized groups.

Applications
Some contemporary applications of social justice architecture include designing buildings and spaces that are accessible to all, and that provide resources and support to marginalized groups, and designing to address ecological issues.

46

DOMESTICITY
**Engaging with the spatial politics
of home and dwelling**

Types
Cohousing is a community where people share common spaces and responsibilities. This shared way of life can reduce the alienation that often comes with domestic labor in traditional domestic settings.

Collective kitchens are shared spaces where people can cook together. This allows people to spend less time having to perform all the traditional domestic tasks associated with private kitchens and more time on other things, and also helps build community.

Collective care spaces are communal living spaces or social condensers (see 67) designed to support systems for care and work, or for the better distribution of care work across communities or society at-large.

Applications
Critiques of domesticity can employ architectural, social, economic, and political knowledge to question and challenge current and historical conditions of the home. These critiques consider how social and economic factors, including class, caste, race, disability, tradition, and normative family structures are integrated into questions about gender.

47

CARBON NEUTRAL
**Designing the eradication
of greenhouse gas emissions**

Types
Carbon-neutral (net-zero) buildings and materials have no net carbon emissions over their lifetime. This means that the building or material is the result of sourcing, production, manufacturing, construction, and maintenance conditions that eliminate or offset the carbon emissions.

Carbon-negative buildings use materials and design strategies to remove more carbon dioxide from the atmosphere than they emit. This can be done by means of new technologies or strategies that take advantage of nature's cycles, systems, and resources.

Applications
There are a number of ways to achieve carbon neutrality or even carbon negativity. Designs can include renewable materials sourced near the project site, such as bamboo, stone, straw, wool, or wood; and recycled materials that would otherwise end up in a landfill. While it is important for architects to be aware of the carbon footprint of their designs, sustainability should also focus on other important social and environmental factors that are part of the ecological footprint of architecture.

48

REUSE
Making use of already-existing structures

Types
Reusing elements or building components considers the conditions of reclaiming and repurposing parts of an existing structure in the construction of a new, or the adaptation of another already-existing structure. Some examples of reuse include using recycled materials, salvaged components, and prefabricated elements more than once.

Reusing entire buildings or structures is known as *adaptive reuse*. Buildings or structures can be reused as forms of historical or cultural preservation, or as economic and ecological approaches that reduce the need for new construction.

Applications
Reuse in architecture can provide many benefits, but it is important to consider the challenges involved before undertaking a project, as well as the overall suitability of an initial design and construction. With careful planning and design, reuse can help minimize the ecological footprint of architecture while addressing many economic and social factors.

49

BUILDING LIFE CYCLE

Accounting for all the stages of a structure's life span

Types

Planning involves designing a project, feasibility studies, and understanding everything needed from start to finish, including materials and labor.

Production accounts for the extraction of raw materials, their transportation and convertion into construction materials, and the building components.

Construction is the materialization of a building.

Postoccupancy means using and maintaining a building over time, including changing its use if needed, and making sure it keeps working.

End of service includes decommissioning, demolition, repurposing, and reuse of a building or building components.

Applications

Each stage of a project or building's life cycle presents its unique challenges and opportunities. This process of assessing a building's complexities should also consider its many stakeholders and constituencies, and how they are involved or affected in every stage.

50

POST-OCCUPANCY
Considering architecture after a project has been inhabited

Types
Intended postoccupancy deals with the desired, planned, or estimated use of a building. For example, residential intended postoccupancy accounts for the many ways that people, families, communities, managers, or workers interact, adapt, and manipulate living spaces.

Alternative postoccupancy includes all forms of deviations from the intended use of a building. It's a form of reuse. Some examples include office buildings transformed into housing units and coliving spaces, shopping malls adapted to function as schools or community centers, or housing units altered to work as commercial spaces.

Applications
By considering the ways people use and interact with buildings, designers can formulate architectures that are responsive, adaptable, and flexible. Postoccupancy considers that the design and use of buildings is not only determined by planners, designers, and clients, but that the people have the power to take control over the design of their environment.

51
HISTORICAL PRESERVATION
Sustaining historical artifacts, edifices, spaces, and infrastructures

Types
Historical preservation protects buildings and sites of historical significance.

Rehabilitation is restoring a structure or space to its original condition.

Restoration returns a structure to its original appearance.

Reconstruction consists of rebuilding a structure from the ground up.

Monuments are built or identified to commemorate, honor, or remember people, places, ideas, concepts, or events.

Memorials are similar to monuments but focus on the remembrance of historical figures and events.

Applications
Through diverse forms of preservation, restoration, or conservation of artifacts, structures, spaces, or landscapes, historical preservation has many challenges, including what to save or remember, how, and why to do it.

52

BIOMIMICRY
**Emulating nature's solutions
to problems and challenges**

Types
Formal biomimicry is the study of nature to understand and imitate its forms and shapes. Some examples include the study of whale fins to design better windmills, or pangolin scales to improve facade insulation.

Process biomimicry is the study of nature to understand and imitate its metabolisms, and cycles. Examples include studying plants to make better solar panels and irrigation systems.

System biomimicry is the study of how nature works as a network of elements with subfunctions, connections, and associations. Examples include the study of ant colonies to develop more efficient communication or transportation systems, and the study of beehives as models for more efficient structures.

Applications
While biomimicry seeks more sustainable, regenerative, and balanced designs, some of its challenges and possibilities lie in the balance between aesthetic and material characteristics, performance, functionality, structural integrity, cost, and material availability.

53
MOBILE ARCHITECTURE
Flexible designs for continuous physical and social motion

Types

Prefabricated mobile architecture is made up of standardized, pre-built parts that can be easily assembled and reconfigured to create flexible, affordable spaces for various uses. These structures are designed to adapt to different environments and needs, allowing for easy updates and replacements over time.

Flexible mobile architecture is meant to be more adaptable than prefabricated modules. It can be constructed with materials that allow for different applications and respond to diverse requirements and conditions.

Moving mobile architecture moves on wheels, on water, and in air.

Applications

As populations expand, there is an increasing need for housing and mixed-use projects that can be quickly and easily assembled in new locations or as appendixes (or parasites) of other already existing structures. Mobile architecture is devised to be rapidly constructed and transformed to satisfy the needs of changing demographics, and growing and shrinking populations.

54

KINETIC ARCHITECTURE
Buildings and structures in motion

Types
Kinetic elements are moving parts of buildings or structures. These can include elements that increase the environmental performance of a building or parts that, through their motion, can allow for a space's transformation.

Kinetic structures are complete projects that move. Some examples include ideal plans for walking buildings or cities, or structures that can be set in motion by wind or air.

Applications
Kinetic architecture is a term used to describe architecture, structures, artifacts, or building components that can move or be set in motion. This can be done through a variety of means, such as wind, water, inertia, or even human power. At the element scale, buildings can be designed to have parts of the structure, facade, or other components move without reducing the structural integrity of the project.

55

AGRITECTURE
Connecting agriculture and architecture

Types

Agribuildings include structures designed for agricultural purposes, such as storing, processing, or housing farm animals or providing agricultural spaces in combination with other uses and programs. Different types of agribuildings can be found on farms and rural areas, but also in towns and cities.

Agrihoods are communities that integrate spaces for agricultural practices as part of a neighborhood. The purpose of agrihoods is to combine spaces for the production of food together with areas for working, living, recreation, and transportation. These neighborhoods can be made up from single-family, multifamily, and mixed-use communities, and be as large as entire cities.

Applications

As the name suggests, agritecture is the combination of agriculture and architecture. As a design practice, philosophy, or approach, to design an agribuilding or agrihood, it is important to consider the needs of a community, the conditions of the site, and the management cycles of the agricultural operations that will take place.

56

FREE SPACE
**Designing for maximum flexibility
and continuous transformation**

Types
Free sections refer to buildings that have spaces that are interconnected
vertically. In this configuration, floors of varying or moving heights, adaptable
circulation elements, and mobile structural elements focus on changing the
vertical dimensions and characteristics of the space.

Free structures are buildings with moving or flexible supporting systems. A
free structure can consist of trusses that are moved by mechanical equipment,
cranes, or kinetically. Free structure and free section can be combined to create
unlimited spatial arrangements in a building.

Applications
While initially designed as general or nonspecific programs, free spaces can
satisfy an array of specific programs. These types of structures can be
convenient in the way they address changing conditions. For example, a free
space can be used as a voting center, a spiritual building, or even as an
emergency shelter or hospital without having to construct a new building.

57

PERIPATETIC ARCHITECTURE

Structures for continuous relocation

Types

Singular peripatetic architectures are individual structures, or varying scales meant for single or collective uses. These nomadic installations can be deployed and installed in many different settings, from forests to deserts.

Collective peripatetic architectures consist of networks of temporary or movable installations that are meant to form an urban or social condition. These types of structures can be found in the form of camps or other forms of social or collective organizations.

Applications

Designed to be easily moved or dismantled and set up again in other locations, some of the materials used by peripatetic architectures include fabrics, textiles, plastics, and composite materials. Because of their flexibility and adaptability, peripatetic architectures can be used in many settings, including ecological dwellings, temporary music festivals, circuses, refugee camps, military installations, pop-up medical clinics, and even outer space exploration.

58

NON-EXTRACTIVIST ARCHITECTURE

Rejecting resource extraction for architecture

Types

Nonextractivist conditions question the current state of architecture and construction, material and resource extraction, and architecture's effects on society and the environment.

Replenishing conditions differ from nonextractivist approaches because they go beyond and aim to replenish environmental, ecological, and social conditions damaged by the construction of buildings.

Applications

Nonextractivist architecture is a type of architecture that does not rely on the removal of natural resources from its original sites. This means that it does not use materials that have been directly mined, logged, or otherwise taken from the earth. Nonextractivist architecture has the potential of reducing the carbon footprint of buildings, repairing some of the construction industry's environmental damage, and creating fairer social conditions. Nonextractivist architectures require a complete retooling and reframing of design, social, economic, and political objectives.

59

WEATHER ARCHITECTURE

Spatial interventions incorporating atmospheric phenomena

Types

Weather buildings are overall structures that contain one or several climatic conditions. These buildings are usually made of structural and technological infrastructures that provide support to the production of weather conditions.

Weather rooms are smaller interventions where different atmospheric or climatic conditions are generated. These spaces can be designed to be inside weather buildings or as freestanding structures.

Weather landscapes are outdoor areas that have been designed to experience or interact with varying climatic conditions.

Applications

Through different methods, strategies, and technologies, weather architectures can treat climate as a building tool, construction material, and spatial conditioner. Weather architecture can be used for scientific research, environmental protection, or creative design. These buildings can clean the environment, support wildlife, and create unique structures inspired by the weather.

60

RECOVERY ARCHITECTURE

Design for the aftermath of natural, human, and ecological crises

Types

Generalized recovery architectures are often prefabricated, predesigned, or modular structures, and components that can be rapidly assembled on-site. To consider the future conditions arising from crisis, these architectures are based on previous data and information from similar events and can be deployed in many different settings.

Site-specific recovery architectures are structures constructed with locally sourced materials that are easy to find. The use of local materials can be an essential factor for many occasions, as imported supplies can be difficult to obtain in the immediate aftermath of a crisis.

Applications

Recovery architecture must strike a balance between speed and quality. In many cases, temporary structures will need to be quickly erected to provide shelter for displaced people, plants, or animal species. Some recovery architectures can have mechanical or architectural features for special uses, such as food storage and preparation, and medical services.

61

UNIVERSALIST DESIGN
Designing accessibility for the many ways of existing in the world

Types
Universalist material design focuses on the characteristics and properties of exterior and interior environments and objects, manufacturing processes, and their asymmetrical effects on different populations depending on their abilities and capabilities.

Universalist experiential design engages with the ways design, interfaces, software, processes, and spaces consider multiple sensory and communication conditions and abilities.

Universalist institutional design engages with rules, regulations, and policies, and focuses on design, planning, regulatory processes, and accountability.

Applications
Through the legal recognition of "disability" as a protected class and the codification of "ergonomic" norms, a limited range of interventions were standardized in certain spheres of life (public property, workplaces, education, multifamily housing). As it seeks to revert forms of exclusion everywhere from buildings to software design and policy making, universalist design cannot be reduced to code compliance, statistical solutions, symbolic gestures, and designer-user binaries.

62

TRANSCALARITY
**Considering multiple scales and
sizes of functions and programs**

Types
Macro-scale transcalarity emphasizes the overall behavior of an architectural
system or network made up of elements of varying scales. This approach
considers how multiple structures and infrastructures correlate and how they
are affected by smaller components and elements.

Micro-scale transcalarity focuses on changes happening at the smallest of
scales. While architecture is usually thought of as buildings, this transcalar
approach engages with design factors that deal with particles, organic matter,
fluids, and fungi.

Applications
Transcalarity invites a holistic approach that considers the multiple scales,
variables, components, and elements that make up the environment. By using a
transcalar approach, designers can think about the complex ways in which small
decisions have big impacts, and how even particles that cannot be seen at plain
sight can have enormous effects on people's quality of life and on the health of
entire ecosystems.

63

INCLUSIVE DESIGN

Designing for everyone, regardless of age, circumstance, and ability

Types

Togetherness designs account for as many different and diverse groups of people as possible.

Fluid interface designs allow for immediate reconfiguration to respond to people's needs.

Automation and control designs integrate digital and mechanical devices that allow for different people to adapt and change their space.

Customization disregards concepts like average or normalcy to provide designs that can be changed and made to cater to specific needs and desires.

Applications

While inclusive design seeks to create a world that is more accessible and welcoming for everyone, designers must be aware that there are many different conditions that affect people in varied ways. Designers should be able to think about spatial layouts, fitting design elements, and safety, comfort, flexibility, and adaptability, but also be aware of the many customs, sensibilities, and ways of relating to one another, as well as the environment.

64

SILVER/CHILDREN'S ARCHITECTURE

Architecture for people at different stages of their lives

Types

Silver architecture is designed to be more accessible and accommodating for people who are older in age. This is accomplished not only by providing architectural and spatial components that respond to safety and comfort issues but by fomenting spaces that invite physical and mental well-being, as well as forms of collective and individualized care.

Children's architecture can include playful spatial sequences and layouts, structures that foment discovery and curiosity, as well as different features that can tap into the many developmental stages of infants and kids.

Applications

Silver and children's architecture can be combined successfully by creating spaces where different age groups complement each other. In architectural terms, silver and children's architecture can be achieved by making alterations to already-existing architectures, or by creating new designs to account for different experiences, sensibilities, and safety requirements.

65

ANIMAL-CENTERED DESIGN

Design for behaviors, conditions, and characteristics of animal species

Types

Habitecture, a combination of habitat and architecture, explores the integration of wildlife habitats into constructed environments. Here, architectures can be used in combination with other constructed artifacts, structures, and spaces. Habitectures can be used for temporary shelter or for permanent housing, with or without human interventions and maintenance.

Autonomous animal architectures are designed to be fully reclaimed by animals and remain disconnected from further intentional human interaction. These types of architectures can be prefabricated and installed in many different places and ecosystems. The materials used to construct autonomous animal-centered architectures may need to replicate the natural ecosystems of the species they are meant to serve.

Applications

Animal-centered habitats need careful planning. Factors like noise, light, and safety for all living beings involved must be considered. These structures should be able to withstand extreme climates and very little or no maintenance, and respect animals' need for independence.

66

COMMONING
Spatial design for the sharing of resources and experiences

Types

Networks of solidarity is the part of commoning that focuses on patterns of collaboration, cooperation, and sharing.

Acts of provisioning in commoning practices seek to satisfy the collective and individual needs of people by collectively produced things and services.

Forms of communal governance encapsulates the way in which commoners or members of the community develop, implement, monitor, and adjust their self-established regulations. If networks of solidarity are the system of commoning, and acts of provisioning is the economic model, communal governance takes care of the political aspect of the community.

Applications

Commoning consists of a series of relationships established and mediated by the sharing of spaces and resources. It challenges centralized (top-down) and capitalist planning, and rejects accumulation of wealth, resources, and land as its goal. Commoning practices propose alternative forms of interpersonal and collective relationships by using architecture as a medium for social exchanges based on reciprocity and solidarity.

67

SOCIAL CONDENSER
Projects designed for large social gatherings

Types

Interior social condensers are spaces within a building that are designed to host several dissimilar programs to encourage social interaction and collaboration. This communal form of interior architecture can consist of a full-level interior within a larger structure, a bridge that connects separate towers or buildings, or an entire building that, through the use of architectural elements and programs, fosters a dynamic set of human relationships.

Exterior or outdoor social condensers are public or communal spaces where people can gather and interact. Outdoor social condensers can take the form of parks, public squares, reclaimed vacant lots, streets, or unfinished structures that have been layered with programs to encourage dynamic coexistence of activities, events, and interactions.

Applications

Social condensers are architectures of public density. Instead of being defined by a singular architectural typology, form, or program, social condensers rely on the mixture of dissimilar activities that aim to generate dynamic social communities.

68

PARTICIPATORY DESIGN

Designing by the exchange of ideas and collective deliberation

Types

Community-based participatory design is a type of nonhierarchical design process that involves working with members of a group or community to design spaces, programs, or structures that meet their needs.

User-centered design focuses on the particular requirements and expectations of the people who will be using the space and designing the space accordingly.

Applications

Participatory design gathers the input of many different constituencies in the design process of a project. As it mediates relationships between different people in search of design consensus, participatory design can help build trust and understanding between people with different interests in a project. There are several benefits to using participatory design as it can help create designs that respond to the people while creating a sense of empowerment as people are more likely to benefit from designs that take their input into consideration.

69

GRID
**Determining spatial paraments
by networks of lines**

Types
Regular grids are a type of layout in which elements are arranged in evenly spaced rows and columns. These grids can be used to create patterns and repetition, find structural logic, or act as an underlying organizational or relational system.

Irregular grids follow a more organic, free-flowing layout. These grids can use asymmetry and uneven spacing between lines to form unique spaces and regulating patterns. Irregular grids can be used to generate random-looking layouts and to produce dynamic and varied types or relationships between the elements collocated on the grid.

Applications
A grid is an organizing principle and system of visible or invisible intersecting lines that form a network of compartmentalization, adjacencies, and immediacies. The grid sets spatial relationships by determining where structures and infrastructures are placed in relation to each other across different scales from small artifacts and objects to entire landscapes and zones.

70

POST-DOMESTIC ARCHITECTURE
Spaces that facilitate life without labor related to the home

Types
Genderless architectures challenge the traditional use of spaces in the home that reinforce traditional binary roles between men and women. These architectures consider the type of physical and emotional labor associated with the nuclear, heteronormative home and formulate alternative forms of architecture based on different forms of relationships between people and society.

Nonexploitative architectures challenge conventional ideas about work, labor, value, the nuclear family, gender, and capitalist production and accumulation. At the same time, some of the concepts explored by this approach include mutual aid, collectivity, refusal to work, nonbinary space, and noncapitalist production.

Applications
Post-domesticity is a field of exploration that has both conceptual and material effects on architecture. From kitchenless architectures to spaces for commoning (see 66) to social condensers (see 67), many forms of spatial organization seek to establish relationships among people that are not based on exploitation, extraction, and subjugation by means of gender, race, class, or (dis)ability.

71

EPHEMERAL ARCHITECTURE

Design that is transient and leaves no physical mark

Types

Inflatable and pneumatic architectures are air-filled or gas-filled structures made out of a variety of materials, including fabric and plastics.

Organic matter architectures are made up of plants, dirt, or even animal skins and furs. After assembly, some of these structures can be made to be movable (see 57) or to disappear over time without needing disassembly.

Paper architectures are made out of paper or cardboard and include anything from simple models to complex buildings and are often used as recovery architectures (see 60). *Paper architectures* is also a term used to describe a historical strategy deployed by architects who refuse to participate in society as an act of protest and as a form of withholding their labor.

Applications

Ephemeral architectures have a range of uses, including fairs, festivals, spiritual rituals, scientific research, ecosystem habitat, or temporary shelter in various environmental conditions.

72

PHENOMENOLOGY

**Design approach that considers
and centers on experience**

Types

Genius loci ("spirit of place") is used in architecture to describe a building or space that has a strong sense of place and identity. This can be achieved through a variety of design elements, such as the use of local materials, traditional forms and patterns, and a connection to the natural environment.

Personal or individual forms of phenomenology refer to the subjective experience of an individual, including one's own thoughts, feelings, and perceptions in relationship to their surroundings.

Collective phenomenology explores the role of group consciousness and perception in shaping experiences of the built environment.

Applications

Phenomenology allows designers to imagine the potential emotional, psychological, and physical experiences that people can have in their buildings and spaces. Different approaches to phenomenology can also help create different experiences in architecture.

73

ARCHITECTURE OF ISOLATION
Spatial design that avoids collective human interactions

Types
Consensual architectures of isolation are structures or systems that people choose to isolate themselves within. This can be for a variety of reasons, including contemplation or meditation. Consensual architectures of isolation can take many forms, such as remote retreats and even virtual spaces.

Nonconsensual architectures of isolation are structures or systems designed to separate individuals from one another without their consent. These architectures of controlled access include prison cells or units for solitary confinement.

Applications
Whether as a voluntary retreat or as a form of punishment, architectures of isolation can have many different spatial characteristics. Many contemplation and meditation architectures of isolation accentuate their relationship with their surroundings and are often found surrounded by landscapes. On the contrary, other antisocial architectures of isolation may eliminate any form of relationship with its surroundings. These architectures are at the center of many discussions about the ethical use of architecture (see 92).

74

DEFENSIVE ARCHITECTURE
Spaces and structures that protect against attacks

Types

Freestanding defensive architectures are different types of fortifications. These structures use durable materials and geometries to present a form of resistance to expected attacks.

Cluster defensive architectures are groups of structures that create a defensive system by association. These structures can have varying sizes, functions, and even materials.

Moving defensive architectures are wheeled, floating, or flying structures. Some of these structures can be designed over rails or as part of complex mechanical or hydraulic systems that allow them to change forms or positions.

Applications

Defensive architectures are designed to protect, withstand, and deflect different attacks or accidents. Designed for military conflict, social unrest, and environmental events, these structures or buildings can operate as models of stealth or to react or prevent their destruction by violent forces and events.

75
SIMULATION DESIGN
Models reproducing architectural and contextual conditions

Types

Discrete event simulation is a way to predict how things will happen over time. It breaks events down into steps and looks at them one at a time. For example, architects use it to see how a building might react to an earthquake.

Process simulation is the use of computer models to replicate the behavior of real-world processes, like understanding how a building will function, or the flow of traffic.

Dynamic simulation is the process of creating a model that can predict the behavior of a system over time. It can be used in architectural design to predict how a building will respond to various loads and environmental conditions, among other uses.

Applications

With many uses and applications, simulation design can help planners, architects, policy makers, urbanists, activists, researchers, and historians better understand buildings, structures, cities, and landscapes.

76

AI CITIES
**Machines or computers performing
urban tasks and decision-making**

Types
Essential services models focus on providing transportation, health care, education, and surveillance or public safety.

Smart transportation models aim at improving transportation options and infrastructure, including services such as ride-sharing, bike-sharing, and public transportation.

Broad spectrum models emphasize civic participation and urban services like water, sewage, and waste management and seek technological solutions like clean energy, smart lighting, and environmental protection.

Business ecosystem models use digital information and communication technologies, skills, and knowledge to stimulate economic activity.

Applications
As governments and private technology producers collaborate and compete for control, questions about limited privacy, excessive network reliance, militarization, accountability, public involvement, and consent are raised.

77

SELF-GENERATING ARCHITECTURE

Structures producing building components and elements on-site

Types

Synthetic self-generating architectures employ machine learning and automated three-dimensional printing technologies to manufacture components using a wide range of synthetic materials including plastics, fiber filaments, and cementitious materials.

Biotechnological self-generating architectures use organic matter and processes to construct parts or entire structures. These structures can use digital and artificial intelligence technology in combination with natural materials.

Applications

Self-generating architecture uses technology or biotechnology to produce and repair buildings, elements, and components. This means that the architecture can create its own form and structure without the need for human intervention. In addition to be custom-designed and built efficiently, these structures can be used for research, testing new materials, and exploring dangerous environments like extreme weather, toxic wastelands, and space.

78

AUTHORLESS ARCHITECTURE

Collective design processes against singular authorship

Types

Collective architectural design not only is produced by groups of people (as much of architecture is) but also recognizes the collective aspect of the process of design. This type of practice also engages with historical forms of architectural knowledge that are passed through generations.

Automated architectural design is the process of using computers to gather historical data and generate architectural designs. This can include everything from generating initial sketches to creating detailed plans and specifications.

Applications

Instead of crediting individuals with design propositions, authorless architecture accepts that architecture is a collective practice and a form of knowledge that is exchanged and passed through time, from generation to generation, and across different cultures. By recognizing that there is a vast array of design options, materials, and processes that make up the complex and rich history of architecture, authorless design can make more sensible design decisions that are not based on ideas of newness or creative uniqueness.

79

DESIGN-BUILD
**Performing every part of the process,
from design to construction**

Types
Builder-led design-build consists of an agreement with a contractor that
becomes the primary contact and primary organizer and executor of the design
and construction.

Designer-led design-build puts the designers as the primary organizers and
performers of the design and construction work. Designers can also take an
active role in providing design and construction services when needed.

Automated design-build replaces the traditional role of designer and builder
with artificial intelligence and automated manufacturing processes. This type of
AI process can be part of future plans of AI cities or be executed in places where
people are absent.

Applications
Design-build establishes a working method and relationship in which a team
of designers and builders develop all the stages of the project from design to
construction. In this process, tasks and disciplines are blurred, as designers may
become builders, construction workers, planners, and strategists.

80

BUILDING CONSTRUCTION MORATORIUM
Imposed or voluntary restriction of the construction of architecture

Types
Temporary building construction moratoriums are legal orders that prohibit or restrict the construction of new buildings in a specific area.

Permanent building construction bans are legal or self-imposed orders that stop and prohibit all construction activity in a specific area.

Applications
Building construction moratorium is the conscious decision, collective choice, or legal action to stop building architecture. Moratoriums can be implemented for a variety of reasons. They can respond to social and environmental demands or prevent further damage to historical or archaeological sites. In some cases, moratoriums may be put in place to give city planners time to develop new zoning regulations and may even result in the permanent banning of building construction. As an environmental and economic critique, building construction moratoriums or bans can argue that there are enough buildings in the world to host all programs that are needed.

81

UTOPIA

**Architectures of ideal or cautionary
societies, cities, and states**

Types

Utopian architecture often portrays the material objectives of a society with ideal
laws, government, and social conditions. When utopia is mentioned in architectural
discussions, it often implies attempts to create perfect societies or the eradication
of everything that doesn't fit its ideal characteristics and values.

Dystopian architecture is the architecture of an imaginary negative society.
Characterized by misery, poverty, violence, and ecological spoliation, among
other forms of oppression, dystopian narratives may be informed by some of the
most problematic factors of a society.

Applications

Coming from the Greek word *ou-topos*, the direct translation of utopia is "no
place." Both utopian and dystopian principles of architecture help form visions
of either a perfect society or a nightmarish one. Even if utopias are never truly
achieved, many of their goals could motivate a pursuit that could move societies
closer to more ideal states.

82

FUTURISMS
Projections of futures formed by particular characteristics, ambitions, and desires

Types
Afrofuturism incorporates elements of Black history and culture within Africa and in diasporas around the planet and beyond.

Indigenous futurism express Indigenous perspectives and speculations of the future, present, and past.

Feminist futurism operates at the intersection of gender, race, sexuality, labor, reproduction, technology, and society.

Technofuturism emphasizes the role that industry and technology play in positive or negative visions of the future.

Ecofuturism combines ecological and technological questions with futurism.

Applications
Today, futurisms engage with many critical, ideal, playful, and dynamic alternative paths to the future and account for communities, experiences, and imaginaries that have been historically disenfranchised or endangered by modernity, development, capitalism, and colonialism.

83

ORGANIC ARCHITECTURE

Designing a close relationship between architecture and the land

Types

Organic buildings consider their forms and materials and the design of their interiors and exteriors to be an integral part of their surroundings.

Earthscrapers are large-scale organic buildings that find dynamic ways to be part of their environment. These organic architectures integrate farming terraces, locally sourced materials, and renewable systems, where instead of waste, the building and nature are in a constant symbiotic cycle.

Landscape cities are urban plans where both buildings and land are a continuous functional program used for living and recreation, producing food and energy.

Applications

As a design and life philosophy, organic architecture understands that humans are part of nature, as opposed to separate from it; thus, it promotes balance between their constructions, activities, and the rest of nature. In this approach, all elements form part of an organic whole: human activities; integration with the site; relationship between components, details, and fixings; and unified forms of furniture and life practices.

84

QUEER CARTOGRAPHIES
Spatial interventions challenging the role of heteronormative design

Types

Analytical queer cartographies consist of the mapping and identification of cultural, political, and material practices of oppression, sexual and gender exclusion and violence in the city.

Subversive queer cartographies turn the identification of exclusionary spaces and elements into architectures and parts of the city that celebrate queerness and nonheteronormativity.

Queer futurisms include trans, nonbinary, two-spirited, gay, lesbian, and asexual possibilities to explore radically inclusive societies, architectures, and cities of emancipatory futures where all identities are welcome, nourished, and protected.

Applications

One of the goals of queer cartographies is to transform the tools of production and documentation of architecture and urbanism for mapping exclusions, forms of resistances, subversion, and radical inclusion. Queer cartographies can identify the sexual geographies of the city, and develop narratives, critical, and imaginative methodologies and historiographies that center LGBTQ2S+ and nonbinary rights and experiences in their search of collective emancipation.

85

SPACE MAGICIANS

Designing spaces, situations, and experiences through fantasy and ancestral knowledge

Types

Space magicians are sculptors of shapes and makers of situations and sensations responsible for the task of imagining the shape of the future, knowing the weight of the past, and understanding the language of history.

Worldmakers are poet astrologers, producers of food, and connoisseurs of the cycles of the cosmos that oppose colonial chaos and destruction by weaving designs that engage with the landscapes and all the relationships between people and their surroundings, the living and nonliving, with the intent of restoring the world and returning it to its own course.

Applications

While the word *architect* (with its Latin and Greek origins) is associated with a profession or discipline with a particular Eurocentric legacy, and very specific responsibilities and expectations in many parts of the world, concepts like the *space magician* and the *worldmaker* force a reconciliation with design as a broader, more ambitious, and less-defined practice of thinking about the world.

86

METABOLISM
Architectures that grow and adapt like a body

Types

Metabolist oceanic cities are modular structures built on stilts, artificial islands, or platforms that float over water.

Metabolist spatial cities use their adaptable and flexible structures to connect in the air in an effort to to minimize their footprint on the ground.

Metabolist agricultural cities use their modular structures and living cells to grow as part of farmland to avoid the loss of agricultural land to architecture.

Applications

Formulated in the context of postwar Japan, metabolism continues to serve as a model for architectures that grow, adapt, are impermanent, and foment renewal, replacement, and regeneration. These imaginary, adaptable, and flexible structures can provide models to respond to exponential population growth and the construction of buildings made out of reusable building components that can offset the environmental impact of new construction.

87

BRUTALISM
**Raw honesty of materials,
programs, labor, and extraction**

Types
Brutalist architectures use tools of architectural representation and production to address all the forces shaping construction projects and making buildings possible. These projects account for the energy, economies, and politics that make materials like concrete, marble, steel, and glass possible.

Brutalist urbanisms focus on the dynamics that give form to cities around the world. These studies and narratives explain flows of capital, political influence, accumulation of wealth and energy, production of waste, and consumption of resources usually produced somewhere else.

Brutalist landscapes tell the stories of designed nature, the layers of history hidden by trees and lakes, and the politics that make these projects possible.

Applications
Brutalism is an architecture of honest, straightforward aesthetics and forms. Tending to questions of ecological and social justice, brutalist approaches and imaginaries make sure that architecture is held accountable as a central instrument in many human and environmental struggles.

88

AVANT-GARDE
**Experimental approach to design
with the aim of changing the world**

Types
Avant-garde architectures propose to move into the future by breaking out of
the past. These imaginaries rely on technological, material, and conceptual
innovation to decisively mark a distinction with current practices.

Après-garde architectures offer an alternative to the futurist desires of
avant-garde practices by finding new ways to deal with historical material.
Whereas avant-garde practices are focused on newness and marking a clear
difference with the past, après-garde imaginaries dream about reusing
strategies, forms, methods, and processes.

Applications
Historically, avant-garde practices have challenged disciplinary boundaries,
developing philosophies that are manifested in different projects and media.
Some examples include avant-garde practitioners designing posters, buildings,
monuments, stage sets, screenplays, and clothes; writing manifestos; and
organizing public events. Avant-garde practices and imaginaries in architecture
include the ability to push boundaries and challenge convention, as well as
create unique and innovative designs.

89

MODERNITIES
Plans that implement social changes and improve living conditions

Types
Contextual modernities account for practices and imaginaries of communities and groups in relationship to their respective landscapes, territories, and conditions. These modernities are not concerned with expansion and occupation but with self-sustaining communities, regenerative practices, and architectures that protect the living and nonliving.

Universalist modernities refer to the supremacy of a particular form of progress, development, and growth, tied to the idea that a hegemonizing modernity is inevitable and unstoppable.

Pluriversal (planetary) modernities refer to the idea that there is not one single modernity but multiple modernities that exist across the globe. This imaginary accounts for practices of solidarity that account for many of the global struggles, questions, and aspirations.

Applications
Modernities provide designers and people in general with other paradigms that can confront and invite the future without recurring to the usual mechanisms and projects that promote planetary degradation and climate crisis tied to building, deforestation, industry, and extraction.

90

POST-COLONIAL ARCHITECTURE

Mitigating the impact of colonization and reimagining life without it

Types

Postcolonial imaginaries (written as one word) are practices that address the architectures of newly formed nation-states as they move outside of colonial control. The postcolonial deals with the realities and emancipatory imaginations of life after the colony.

Post-colonial imaginaries (hyphenated) explore how the brutal systems used on Caribbean plantations have spread globally. It examines how colonial-style power and control have become widespread, and how the ideas of survival, resistance, and freedom born from colonial struggles can help address today's global challenges.

Applications

To imagine what is possible within and beyond the colonial condition, designers and planners have to understand and communicate with the past, while proposing new imaginaries of emancipation, sovereignty, community, and empowerment. The postcolonial addresses public space, institutional buildings and programs, urban logic, energy and sustainability, wealth accumulation, and relationships to the landscapes and to resource extraction.

91

PANOPTICON
Spatial conditions of continuous surveillance

Types

Digital panopticon accounts for the cybernetic networks of surveillance that have become present in all spheres through computers, smartphones, and the presence of the Internet.

Physical panopticon entails all the material and architectural manifestations of cultures of surveillance and control. Surveillance in this case is connected to concepts of security and private property.

Applications

Taking its name from the studies on an ideally surveilled prison, the panopticon has come to signify the omnipresence of architectures of control. A critique of the panopticon raises awareness against a culture and architecture of surveillance that documents increasing aspects of life as technology develops. Architectures concerned with the contemporary reach of the panopticon culture create ways of living beyond invasive surveillance technologies and their connection to the growing footprint of the prison and military industrial complex.

92

ABOLITIONIST ARCHITECTURE
Design for the end of slavery, prisons, and other oppressive institutions

Types
Restorative justice aims to restore society to its state before it was harmed and broken by injustice and oppression. The architectures of restorative justice focus on reparations and fixing broken elements of society.

Transformative justice seeks to radically change and transform communities so that the harm cannot happen again. Transformative architectures imagine other worlds based on justice, community, and emancipation.

Applications
Abolitionist architecture is based on the principle that prisons are the continuation of models of chattel slavery, and that by abolishing them, society would have addressed one of the most pervasive forms of structural human oppression. Instead of proposing the design of better, more efficient, and humane prisons, jails, detention centers, or any architectural form of nonconsensual isolation (see 73), abolitionism believes that society should invest its resources on forms of social support and welfare that make prisons unnecessary.

93

ANTI-RACIST ARCHITECTURE

Design that exposes and subverts racist practices and processes

Types

Anti-racist and anticasteist architectures consider the links between race, caste, and the subjugation and oppression of people by means of the materialization of legal and economic systems. Anti-racist and anticasteist architectures question, subvert, and oppose architecture as a tool for control, domination, subjugation, extraction, and oppression.

Abolitionist architectures (see 92) seek the elimination of imprisonment, policing, and surveillance while creating lasting alternatives. This approach recognizes the relationship between slavery and its legacy in the modern prison system.

Applications

Anti-racist architecture seeks to dismantle all racist monuments, mechanisms of exploitation, accumulation of wealth, and objectification and commodification of bodies and replace them with truly equitable, fair, and dignifying spaces. Anti-racist imaginaries understand the relationship between deforestation; the desecration, occupation, and destruction of Indigenous territories; and the construction of systems of value that spoliate the environment, and seek forms of ecological and social justice that make the world a better place.

94

FEMINIST CITY
Design that addresses the needs of women and nonbinary and trans people

Types

Intersectional or interlocking imaginaries address how design deals with issues of race, caste, gender, (dis)ability, and class. This approach takes into account the intersections or interlocking of different forms of oppression when thinking about the city and its potential alternatives.

Transfeminist imaginaries in the context of the city focus on articulating forms of social resistance that preserve feminist rights while integrating mobility between genders, bodies, and sexualities.

Applications

The feminist city encompasses many different feminist critiques of the planned and built environment. In more specific terms, to think about the city through a feminist approach, which is intersectional, interlocking, and trans, accounts for the affirmative coexistence of differences in a space where labor, care, safety, and community are central to architectural spaces and the relationships, connections, and practices they enhance. In the form of a design philosophy and practice, a transfeminist approach creates safe spaces of transit from place to place, and from identity to identity.

95

SELF-SUSTAINING ARCHITECTURE

Addressing all aspects of maintenance and sustenance of architecture

Types

Eco-architectures tackle self-sustenance at the scale of a building. A truly ecological architecture accounts for all the scales and forms of interaction, from building materials to energy strategies to the social programs that the buildings provide. An eco-architecture is a node in a larger network of strategies of self-sustenance and sovereignty.

Eco-cities take all the principles of eco-architecture and apply them to the scale of community and society. Self-sustaining eco-cities are designed to minimize the impact of human life on the rest of ecologies while creating the infrastructures that foment systems that protect people and the environment.

Applications

As the climate crisis becomes more imminent, the possibility of self-sustaining architectures becomes more urgent. While technological advancements make the incorporation of photovoltaic panels and wind-powered turbines more common, self-sustaining architectures have existed long before any of these devices were developed.

96

VIRTUAL CITY
**Design of urban conditions
that exists solely on computers**

Types
Virtual simulations are digital worlds that imitate behaviors, patterns, and logics found in reality. These fully immersive and participatory virtual environments are also called *metaverses*, or digital worlds that imitate reality. Metaverses have not only cities but also different environments like landscapes with realistic features like grass, rain, rivers, and insects.

Virtual utopias depict unrealistic environments that don't necessarily respond to or imitate reality. Some characteristics of virtual utopias might include being able to choose one's own appearance, have superhuman abilities, fly, and visit different planets or dimensions.

Applications
Virtual cities are places that exist in the notional environment of communication over computer networks of cyberspace. As technologies progress, virtual cities can be used for planning purposes to test different scenarios and see what works best before implementing changes in the real world.

97

PLAYGROUND CITY

**Conceiving spaces for play,
where humans are players**

Types

Architectures for organized play consist of designs that stimulate play through rules and constraints. These architectures lay out boundaries and parameters that make collective or individual play possible in the playground city. Organized play is the closest thing to a sport.

Architectures for spontaneous play are artifacts, elements, spaces, and structures that stimulate the possibility of play. In the playground city, people are free to play whenever they desire, alone and in groups. These architectures make that possible.

Applications

In the playground city, all people are the players. To imagine a city devised for playing requires the consideration of many different age groups, sensibilities, bodily capacities, and abilities of all members of the community. This philosophy is based on the idea that play can make people's lives better by providing them with the space and time to have fun and joy, both alone and in community.

98

RELATIONALITY

Design for relations between species, the living, and the nonliving

Types

Flat ontologies offer explanations of the world that do not contain any hierarchy or center. In a flat ontology, humans are not at the center of the world, and Earth is not at the center of the universe, but rather are all part of a network of things.

Object-oriented ontologies study the world and the cosmos while maintaining that everything is objects and relations, and relations between objects. In this philosophy, objects and hyperobjects, or very big objects, affect many other objects.

Applications

Both flat ontologies and object-oriented ontology are useful fields of knowledge for architecture in relationship to sustainability and ecology, as they help understand the interconnectedness of things and the importance of even the most minuscule objects and ungraspable phenomena. As designers take into account the relationships between different elements, they should be able to make better-informed decisions that consider the long-term impacts of every action, project, or plan.

99

PLANETARY DESIGN

Design philosophy that tackles challenges at the scale of the planet

Types

Atmospheric design deals with all the components that allow the environment to be conducive to life. This can include everything from the emissions connected to the construction industry to renewable building technologies.

Oceanic design focuses on how the oceans are affected by development and industry. This accounts not only for what happens directly on bodies of water but for how atmospheric and geological changes alter its life and ecologies.

Geodesign emphasizes geomorphological processes and how Earth is impacted by resource extraction and alterations linked to architecture, construction, and industry.

Applications

Planetary designers think about how each project relates to poverty, health, security, life, and sovereignty. Through the understanding of the multiple factors that make life possible on Earth, these designers aim to produce more sensible designs that account for the footprint of architecture, not only in the moment but for future generations.

100

INTERGALACTIC DESIGN

**Speculative and scientific
design of structures in space**

Types
Interplanetary architectures are designs that address the particular characteristics
of other planets.

Intergalactic architectures imagine the extreme conditions and technologies
needed for traveling across galaxies.

Interuniversal architectures deal with theories about the multiverse that include
an infinite number of universes, each with their own laws of physics, and the
possibility of parallel universes with many alternative versions of this universe.

Applications
Thinking about intergalactic architecture and imagining what it's like to live
and explore the dimension beyond planet Earth can have some advantages for
designers. By addressing compact and austere living conditions, including new
technological advances, and accounting for many of the questions of theoretical
physics, designers can come up with new architectural propositions.

ACKNOWLEDGMENTS

The Pocket Universal Principles of Architecture is a pocket-sized experiment to create a popular literacy of the built, destroyed, and imagined environment . . .

We would like to thank . . .

Jonathan Simcosky, David Martinell, and the team at Rockport Publishers and Quarto Books

Alice Grandoit-Šutka, Justin Garrett Moore, Francisco Javier Rodríguez, Aaron Betsky, Aki Ishida, Mark Raymond, Jess Myers, Ilze Wolff, Alexandra Pagán, Roque Raquel Salas Rivera, Aki Ishida, Luis Rico Gutierrez, Samia Henni, Isabel Flower+Midori, and Julio Ramos

Dan J. Roche, Abdul Qutub, Tamar Shafrir, and Samiha Meem

Post-Novis / Luis Othoniel Rosa + Hilary Wiese + Holly Craig + Ophelia S. Chan + Rose Florian + Coco Allred + Christopher Rey Perez

Our colleagues and friends/ and our fantastic students at Iowa State University / Columbia University / University of Illinois Urbana-Champaign / Virginia Tech / Carnegie Mellon University / University of Nebraska-Lincoln / The School of Architecture at Taliesin / and all around the world

Great Plains Action Society + Sikowis Nobiss + Shelley Buffalo

And the amazing Eyden Jaheim and Ema Yuizarix . . .

Nathalie Frankowski &
Cruz Garcia with their child,
Ema Yuizarix.

www.waithinktank.com

ABOUT THE AUTHORS

WAI Architecture Think Tank is a planetary studio practicing by questioning the political, historical, and material legacy and imperatives of architecture and urbanism. Founded by Puerto Rican architect, artist, curator, educator, author, and theorist Cruz Garcia and French architect, artist, curator, educator, author, and poet Nathalie Frankowski, WAI is one of their several forms of public engagement that include the free and alternative education platform and trade-school LOUDREADERS and the antidisciplinary collective Post-Novis.

Garcia and Frankowski are Associate Professors at Iowa State University, where they are Design for Critical Futures Fellows in Activism and Emancipatory practice, respectively, and faculty at the Advanced Architectural Design program at Columbia University in New York City. Their work has been part of exhibitions at the Centre Pompidou Metz, Neues Museum Nuremberg, Museum of Art, Architecture, and Technology Lisbon, Museum of Modern Art New York, the Chicago Architecture Biennial, and the Venice Architecture Biennale.

They are authors of *The Pocket Universal Principles of Architecture*, *Universal Principles of Architecture: 100 Archetypes, Methods, Conditions, Relationships, and Imaginaries*, *Narrative Architecture: A Kynical Manifesto*, *Pure Hardcore Icons: A Manifesto on Pure Form in Architecture*, and *A Manual of Anti-Racist Architecture Education*.

Modernities are different ideas about progress and the future.

Modularity refers to set systems of repeating elements.

Monumentality are grand gestures of power, control, abundance, or wealth.

Movements describe significant artistic periods.

Perspectives are drawings or images that simulate depth.

Plan drawings are two-dimensional representations of a project or space.

Planning is the preparation process for an action or design.

Poché are areas of an architectural drawing that are filled with a solid color.

Prefab or **prefabricated** means manufactured parts to be put together.

Program responds to the use, utilization, or activities of a building or space.

Scale is a reference system used to compare the size of things.

Section displays a cut through the body of a volume.

Style means features that make a project look like it belongs to a certain group.

Suburban are areas of lower density and with less mixture of programs.

Symmetry is the balanced or similar parts facing each other or around an axis.

Tabula rasa is the belief that there's a blank canvas to start a project.

Typology uses similar characteristics to classify projects.

Urban describes conditions of collective human inhabitation in cities, and towns.

Urbanism studies cities, towns, and other forms of collective human inhabitation.

GLOSSARY

Asymmetry is the dissimilar arrangement of parts.

Axonometry is a parallel projection of a three-dimensional object.

Collage juxtaposes and overlays images to create a new composition.

Context refers to the immediacies surrounding a project.

Elements or *components* are parts of buildings or spaces like columns or walls.

Extraction is the removal of resources from the earth.

Fabrication is the manufacturing of components or parts.

Facade is visible face, wall, or component of a structure.

Fenestrations are openings in walls, like windows or doors.

Formal describes the shape, or figure of an element, component, or structure.

Gentrification displaces and replaces people with more affluent ones.

High-tech incorporates advanced technologies in design.

Infrastructures are necessary underlying systems, elements, and utilities.

Landscape is the areas of land that include elements, vegetation, structures, and buildings.

Models are digital and physical objects made to study a design.

Modernism is a movement that used industrially-produced new materials.